SAFETY FIRST

Safety at School

Joanne Mattern
ABDO Publishing Company

visit us at
www.abdopub.com

Published by Abdo Publishing Company 4940 Viking Drive, Edina, Minnesota 55435.
Copyright © 1999 by Abdo Consulting Group, Inc. International copyrights reserved in all
countries. No part of this book may be reproduced in any form without written permission
from the publisher.

Published 1999
Printed in the United States of America.
Second Printing 2002

Photo credits: Peter Arnold, Inc., SuperStock

Edited by Julie Berg
Contributing editor Morgan Hughes
Graphics by Linda O'Leary

Library of Congress Cataloging-in-Publication Data

Mattern, Joanne, 1963-
    Safety at school / Joanne Mattern.
    p. cm. -- (Safety first)
    Includes index.
    Summary: Discusses how to be safe while in school or going to school, covering
such aspects as being on the bus, walking and biking to school, carrying things
safely, and fire drills.
    ISBN 1-57765-070-0
    1. Schools--Safety measures--Juvenile literature. 2. Safety education--Juvenile
literature. [1. Safety. 2. Schools.] I. Title. II. Series.
    LB2864.5.M38   1999
    363.11'371--DC21   98-5529
                                                               CIP
                                                               AC

Contents

Safety First!

There are a lot of fun things to do at school. You learn new things. You see your friends. You play games at recess and during lunch.

No matter what you do at school, it is important to always stay safe. Staying safe means you won't get hurt. You won't get in trouble. And you will keep other people from getting hurt or in trouble, too!

How can you stay safe in school? The best way is to follow the rules and think before you act. This book will show you many ways to always put safety first while you are at school.

Opposite page:
Help make your school a
safe place to be.

Safety on the School Bus

When you are waiting for the school bus to pick you up, don't stand in the road. Stand on the sidewalk or on the grass. Stay as far away from cars as you can.

If you play ball or other games while you wait for the bus, don't run into the road. Always look out for cars.

Watch for cars when you get on or off the bus, too. If you have to cross the street, make sure all of the cars have stopped first. Wait for the driver, **monitor**, or parent to tell you it is safe to cross.

The best way to stay safe on the bus is to sit in your seat. If your bus has **seat belts**, be sure to wear one.

Always do what the driver tells you. Don't run or throw things inside the bus. The driver should be watching the road, not you!

Stand quietly in line when waiting to board the bus.

Walking and Biking to School

If you walk to school, look out for cars. Be careful when you cross the street or wait at the corner. If there is a **crossing guard** at the corner, don't cross until he or she says it is okay.

If you ride a bike to school, obey traffic laws. You should ride on the side of the road, in the same

This page and opposite page: Wait at a crosswalk until it's safe to cross.

8

direction that traffic is moving. Watch out for people who are walking or crossing the street.

Some neighborhoods aren't very nice to walk through. If you have to pass empty buildings or other places that scare you, try to walk on the other side of the street. Walking with a group of friends is a good way to stay safe and have fun, too.

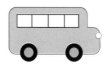

Staying Safe in the Halls

When you get to school, there are many safety rules to follow. One important rule is to not run in the halls. If you run in the halls, you might fall and hurt yourself. You might run into another student and hurt him or her. You might even run into the **principal** and get into trouble!

If your whole class is walking in the halls, stay with the group and do what your teacher tells you. Don't push or shove. That is not only unsafe, it is rude, too!

Opposite page:
Walking in the halls is
safer than running.

Riverdale Elementary Library

Carrying
Things Safely

Running in the halls or in the classroom is a bad idea. It's even worse if you are carrying something. If you are carrying a scissors or another sharp object, you could hurt people if you run into them. You could also hurt yourself if you fall down. The best way to carry a scissors is to hold the closed sharp end away from you and point it down, toward the floor.

This is the safe way to carry scissors.

You should be extra careful if you are holding something that might break, like a glass jar. If you are carrying a glass of water, try not to spill any on the floor. You or someone else could slip in the water and fall. Call a teacher or janitor to clean up spills.

Be careful when working with scissors.

Safety in Gym Class

Gym class is lots of fun. But it isn't much fun if you or someone else gets hurt!

When you are playing games, be sure to follow the rules. Do what the teacher tells you. Make sure you know how to use the **gear**. Don't be afraid to ask questions if you aren't sure how something works.

What should you do if you or someone else gets hurt? Tell the teacher right away. He or she will help the person who is hurt. The teacher might send for the nurse to help, too.

Opposite page:
Follow the rules and use gear
correctly when playing games.

Fire Drills

The bell rings. It's a **fire drill**!

Fire drills might seem silly, but they are important. Everyone needs to know what to do in case there is a real fire.

During a fire drill, the most important thing to do is listen to your teacher. Line up with your class. Then walk outside. Don't stop to take anything with you or try to find your friends. Don't talk. You need to listen to what your teacher tells you.

When you hear the fire alarm, head for the exit with your class.

Once you are outside, stay with your class. Be quiet so you can hear what your teacher says. The teacher or the **principal** will tell you when it is safe to go back inside.

Follow your teacher's directions during a fire drill.

Keeping Things Safe

Not only do you and your friends need to stay safe, but your things need to be safe, too.

If you have a locker, always keep it locked. Don't tell anyone what your locker **combination** is. If no one knows the combination, no one can break in.

If you keep valuables with you at school, make sure they are put away inside your desk. That way, no one will see them and want to take them. If you have something that is very important to you, carry it in your pocket. Never leave money in your desk.

Opposite page:
Keep your locker
combination to yourself.

If You See a Stranger

Most of the people in school belong there. You will see students, teachers, janitors, and other workers in the halls. But sometimes you might see a stranger in school. If you see someone **suspicious** in the halls or on the playground, don't talk to that person. Find a teacher or another adult you know. Tell the adult what you saw. He or she will take care of the problem.

You should also tell a teacher if you see someone acting strangely. It doesn't matter if the person is a student or an adult. The best thing to do is let a teacher take care of things.

If you follow simple rules, you can help make school a safe, fun place for you and your friends. Just remember to always put safety first!

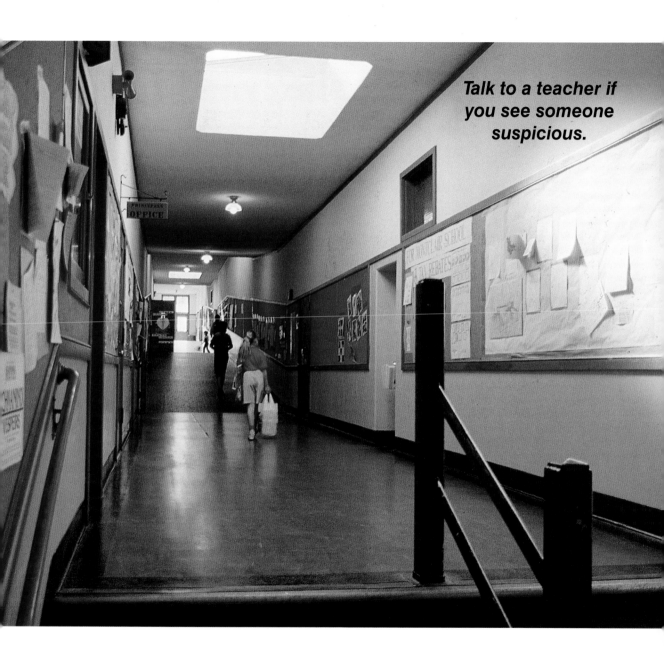

Talk to a teacher if you see someone suspicious.

Glossary

Combination (kom-bin-AY-shuhn) - a series of numbers that open a lock.

Crossing guard (KRAWSS-ing gard) - a person who stops traffic so people can cross the street.

Fire drill - practicing how to get out of a building in case of a fire.

Gear - equipment or clothing like hockey sticks or football helmets used in gym class.

Monitor (MON-uh-tur) - a person who keeps track of other people.

Principal (PRIN-suh-puhl) - the head of a school.

Seat belt - a strap or harness that holds a person in the seat of a car, truck, bus, or airplane in case of an accident.

Suspicious (suh-SPISH-uhss) - the feeling that someone has done something wrong. Or, the feeling that someone shouldn't be there. Someone that looks suspicious may look strange or out of place.

Internet Sites

Bicycling Safety
http://www.cam.org/~skippy/sites/cycling/SafetyLinks.html
Stories, studies, statistics, and tips on everything from safe cycling practices to maintenance. Special interest sections for kids and parents, and links to many interesting sites!

Safety Tips for Kids on the Internet
http://www.fbi.gov/kids/internet/internet.htm
The FBI has set up a "safety tips for the internet" website. It has very good information about how to protect yourself online.

National School Safety Center
http://www.nssc1.org/
This site provides training and resources for preventing school crime and violence.

Home Safety
http://www.safewithin.com/homesafe/
This site helps to make the home more secure, info on the health of the home environment and other safety resources.
These sites are subject to change.

Pass It On

Educate readers around the country by passing on information you've learned about staying safe. Share your little-known facts and interesting stories. Tell others about bike riding, school experiences, and any other stuff you'd like to discuss. We want to hear from you!

To get posted on the ABDO Publishing Company website E-mail us at **"adventure@abdopub.com"**
Download a free screen saver at www.abdopub.com

Index